THE SONGS OF ANDREW LLOYD WEBBER™
40 OF HIS GREATEST HITS

ANDREW LLOYD WEBBER™

Andrew Lloyd Webber™ is a trademark owned by Andrew Lloyd Webber.

ISBN 978-1-4768-1405-6

HAL•LEONARD®
7777 W. BLUEMOUND RD. P.O. BOX 13819 MILWAUKEE, WI 53213

In Australia Contact:
Hal Leonard Australia Pty. Ltd.
4 Lentara Court
Cheltenham, Victoria, 3192 Australia
Email: ausadmin@halleonard.com.au

Visit Hal Leonard Online at
www.halleonard.com

CONTENTS

ALL I ASK OF YOU
from THE PHANTOM OF THE OPERA

VIOLIN

Music by ANDREW LLOYD WEBBER
Lyrics by CHARLES HART
Additional Lyrics by RICHARD STILGOE

Moderately slow

ANOTHER SUITCASE IN ANOTHER HALL
from EVITA

Violin

Words by TIM RICE
Music by ANDREW LLOYD WEBBER

Slowly (8 beat feel)

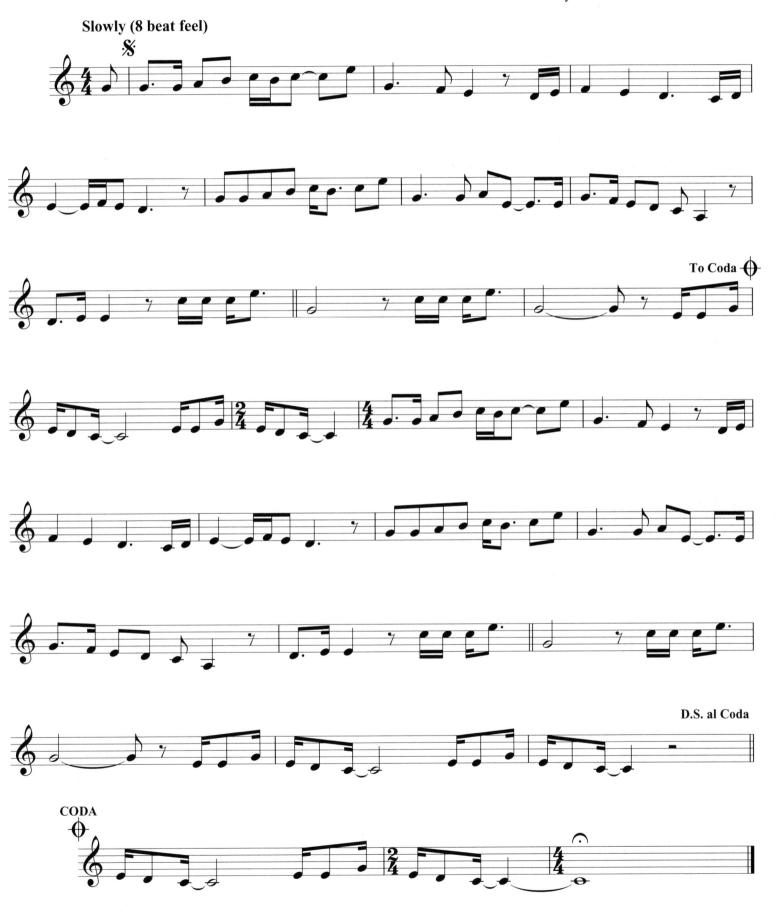

AMIGOS PARA SIEMPRE
(Friends for Life)
(The Official Theme of the Barcelona 1992 Games)

VIOLIN

Music by ANDREW LLOYD WEBBER
Lyrics by DON BLACK

7

ANGEL OF MUSIC
from THE PHANTOM OF THE OPERA

VIOLIN

Music by ANDREW LLOYD WEBBER
Lyrics by CHARLES HART
Additional Lyrics by RICHARD STILGOE

Moderately, in 2

9

ANY DREAM WILL DO

from JOSEPH AND THE AMAZING TECHNICOLOR® DREAMCOAT

Music by ANDREW LLOYD WEBBER
Lyrics by TIM RICE

VIOLIN

AS IF WE NEVER SAID GOODBYE
from SUNSET BOULEVARD

VIOLIN

Music by ANDREW LLOYD WEBBER
Lyrics by DON BLACK and CHRISTOPHER HAMPTON,
with contributions by AMY POWERS

CLOSE EVERY DOOR

from JOSEPH AND THE AMAZING TECHNICOLOR® DREAMCOAT

Violin

Music by ANDREW LLOYD WEBBER
Lyrics by TIM RICE

DON'T CRY FOR ME ARGENTINA

from EVITA

VIOLIN

Words by TIM RICE
Music by ANDREW LLOYD WEBBER

EVERYTHING'S ALRIGHT
from JESUS CHRIST SUPERSTAR

VIOLIN

Words by TIM RICE
Music by ANDREW LLOYD WEBBER

I DON'T KNOW HOW TO LOVE HIM

from JESUS CHRIST SUPERSTAR

Violin

Words by TIM RICE
Music by ANDREW LLOYD WEBBER

HIGH FLYING, ADORED

from EVITA

VIOLIN

Words by TIM RICE
Music by ANDREW LLOYD WEBBER

I AM THE STARLIGHT
from STARLIGHT EXPRESS

VIOLIN

Music by ANDREW LLOYD WEBBER
Lyrics by RICHARD STILGOE

Moderately

I BELIEVE MY HEART

from THE WOMAN IN WHITE

VIOLIN

Music by ANDREW LLOYD WEBBER
Lyrics by DAVID ZIPPEL

21

I'M HOPELESS WHEN IT COMES TO YOU

from STEPHEN WARD

VIOLIN

Music by ANDREW LLOYD WEBBER
Book and Lyrics by DON BLACK
and CHRISTOPHER HAMPTON

LEARN TO BE LONELY
from THE PHANTOM OF THE OPERA

VIOLIN

Music by ANDREW LLOYD WEBBER
Lyrics by CHARLES HART

LIGHT AT THE END OF THE TUNNEL
from STARLIGHT EXPRESS

VIOLIN

Music by ANDREW LLOYD WEBBER
Lyrics by RICHARD STILGOE

LOVE CHANGES EVERYTHING

from ASPECTS OF LOVE

VIOLIN

Music by ANDREW LLOYD WEBBER
Lyrics by DON BLACK and CHARLES HART

MEMORY
from CATS

VIOLIN

Music by ANDREW LLOYD WEBBER
Text by TREVOR NUNN after T.S. ELIOT

Slowly

LOVE NEVER DIES

from LOVE NEVER DIES

Violin

Music by ANDREW LLOYD WEBBER
Lyrics by GLENN SLATER

29

MAKE UP MY HEART

from STARLIGHT EXPRESS

Music by ANDREW LLOYD WEBBER
Lyrics by RICHARD STILGOE

VIOLIN

Moderately

MR. MISTOFFELEES
from CATS

VIOLIN

Music by ANDREW LLOYD WEBBER
Text by T.S. ELIOT

THE MUSIC OF THE NIGHT

from THE PHANTOM OF THE OPERA

VIOLIN

Music by ANDREW LLOYD WEBBER
Lyrics by CHARLES HART
Additional Lyrics by RICHARD STILGOE

NO MATTER WHAT
from WHISTLE DOWN THE WIND

VIOLIN

Music by ANDREW LLOYD WEBBER
Lyrics by JIM STEINMAN

THE PERFECT YEAR

from SUNSET BOULEVARD

Violin

Music by ANDREW LLOYD WEBBER
Lyrics by DON BLACK
and CHRISTOPHER HAMPTON

Moderately

THE PHANTOM OF THE OPERA

from THE PHANTOM OF THE OPERA

Violin

Music by ANDREW LLOYD WEBBER
Lyrics by CHARLES HART
Additional Lyrics by RICHARD STILGOE
and MIKE BATT

PIE JESU
from REQUIEM

VIOLIN

By ANDREW LLOYD WEBBER

Slowly

STARLIGHT EXPRESS

from STARLIGHT EXPRESS

VIOLIN

Music by ANDREW LLOYD WEBBER
Lyrics by RICHARD STILGOE

THE POINT OF NO RETURN

from THE PHANTOM OF THE OPERA

VIOLIN

Music by ANDREW LLOYD WEBBER
Lyrics by CHARLES HART
Additional Lyrics by RICHARD STILGOE

SEEING IS BELIEVING

from ASPECTS OF LOVE

VIOLIN

Music by ANDREW LLOYD WEBBER
Lyrics by DON BLACK and CHARLES HART

(small notes optional)

STICK IT TO THE MAN

from SCHOOL OF ROCK

VIOLIN

Music by ANDREW LLOYD WEBBER
Lyrics by GLENN SLATER

SUPERSTAR
from JESUS CHRIST SUPERSTAR

VIOLIN

Words by TIM RICE
Music by ANDREW LLOYD WEBBER

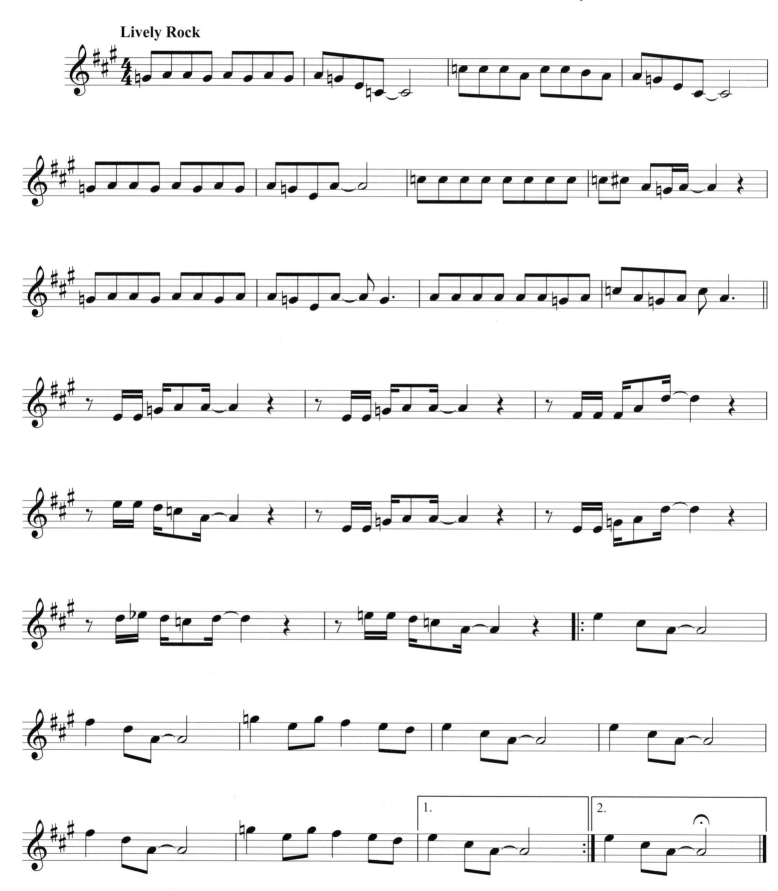

TELL ME ON A SUNDAY

from SONG & DANCE

VIOLIN

Music by ANDREW LLOYD WEBBER
Lyrics by DON BLACK

TAKE THAT LOOK OFF YOUR FACE
from SONG & DANCE

VIOLIN

Music by ANDREW LLOYD WEBBER
Lyrics by DON BLACK

THINK OF ME
from THE PHANTOM OF THE OPERA

VIOLIN

Music by ANDREW LLOYD WEBBER
Lyrics by CHARLES HART
Additional Lyrics by RICHARD STILGOE

'TIL I HEAR YOU SING

from LOVE NEVER DIES

VIOLIN

Music by ANDREW LLOYD WEBBER
Lyrics by GLENN SLATER

UNEXPECTED SONG

from SONG & DANCE

VIOLIN

Music by ANDREW LLOYD WEBBER
Lyrics by DON BLACK

WHISTLE DOWN THE WIND

from WHISTLE DOWN THE WIND

Violin

Music by ANDREW LLOYD WEBBER
Lyrics by JIM STEINMAN

WISHING YOU WERE SOMEHOW HERE AGAIN

from THE PHANTOM OF THE OPERA

VIOLIN

Music by ANDREW LLOYD WEBBER
Lyrics by CHARLES HART
Additional Lyrics by RICHARD STILGOE

WITH ONE LOOK

from SUNSET BOULEVARD

Violin

Music by ANDREW LLOYD WEBBER
Lyrics by DON BLACK and CHRISTOPHER HAMPTON,
with contributions by AMY POWERS

YOU MUST LOVE ME

from the Cinergi Motion Picture EVITA

Words by TIM RICE
Music by ANDREW LLOYD WEBBER

VIOLIN